D1079463

SPLATivity
STICKER BOOK

Where there is a missing sticker, you will see an empty shape. Search the sticker pages to find the missing stickers.

Turn to the back of the book to press out and create an amazing game, stinky code-breakers and even a **SPLAT** box!

make believe ideas

SLiME spotting

Find six differences between the slime machines.

2

Pie SPLAT

Follow the lines to find out who gets a cream pie in their face!

YUCK!

Use stickers and doodles to create a gross and gooey cream pie.

4

FUN at the fair

Find the missing stickers to finish the scene.

Circle the one that doesn't belong on each row.

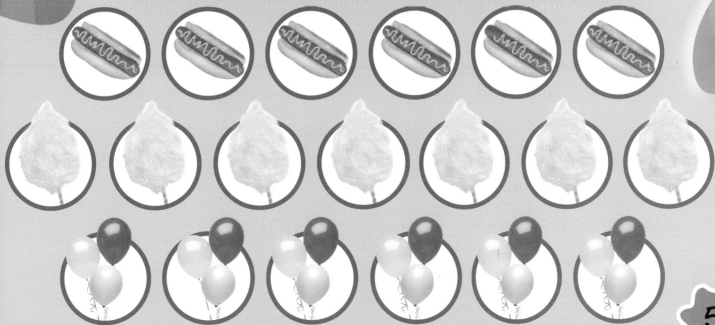

SWAMP MONSTERS

Search the swamp to find the things below. Tick the boxes as you find them.

- [ ] 1 old boot
- [ ] 3 swamp monsters
- [ ] 2 fish
- [ ] 4 dragonflies
- [ ] 3 birds
- [ ] 5 Venus flytraps

SPLAT attack!

Create your own silly splats using stickers, colour and doodles.

We've got **SPLAT**itude!

9

CRAZY codes

1. Press out the letter strip and code-breaker sock from the card pages.

2. Slot the letter strip into the code-breaker. The letters on the letter strip will now line up with different letters on the sock.

3. Crack the codes to reveal the splat names!

RCTDWJ

_ _ _ _ _ _

DAWLEEPC

_ _ _ _ _ _ _ _

CZEETP

_ _ _ _ _ _

QLYRFD

_ _ _ _ _ _

Answers: Grisly, Splatter, Rottle, Fangus

SPLAT city

Find a path through the city.
You must go through every square
once, and avoid the splats!

11

ZOOM-iN ZOO

Draw lines to match each animal to its crazy close-up.

sweeT fix!

Find the missing stickers to fix the sweet machine.

Colour the hungry monsters.

13

SILLY in space

14

I SCREAM for ice cream

Which of these ice creams are on display?
Put a tick next to the ones you can see.

milk and pepper ☐

tomato sauce and popcorn ☐

sausage and chocolate ☐

tuna and cream ☐

pepperoni and lemon ☐

toothpaste and orange juice ☐

Create your own ice cream.
Choose from the list of toppings,
and then draw them on.

- rotten cherries
- mouldy wafer
- chewy worms
- slime sauce
- carrot sticks
- maggot sprinkles

15

Junk JUNGLE

Use stickers to match the piles of junk.

How many splat monsters can you count? Write the answer. ....

In the **air**

sewer scramble

Press out the code-breaker toilet and fold along the crease. Lift the lid to reveal the key and use it to draw a line from start to finish.

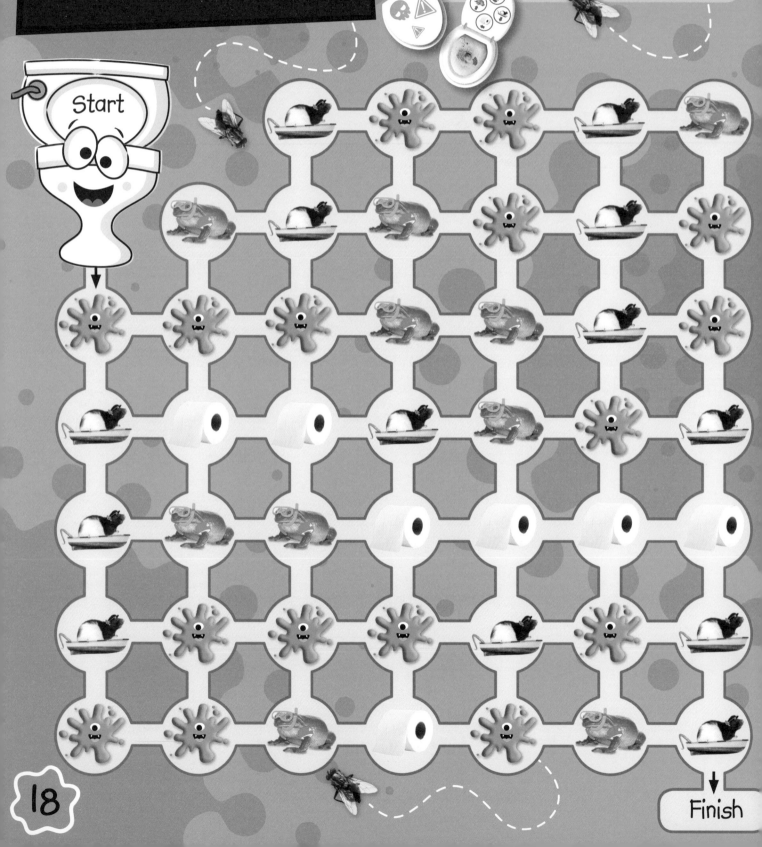

Start

Finish

Jigsaw JUMBLE

Circle the piece that doesn't belong in the puzzle.

Draw a line to match the correct puzzle piece to the empty space.

19

Search and SPLAT

How many of each splat can you find? Write the answers in the circles.

2
....

....

....

....

....

....

....

Runaway SLIME

There's a slime on the loose!

Use the code-breaker sock from the back of your book to reveal the hiding place of the runaway slime.

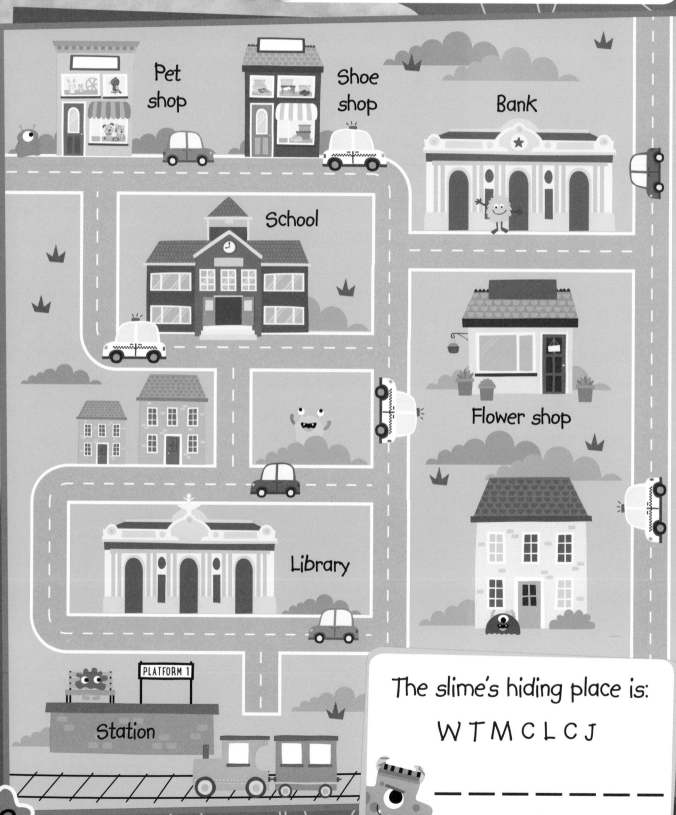

Pet shop		Shoe shop		Bank
School				
			Flower shop	
Library				
Station				

The slime's hiding place is:

W T M C L C J

_ _ _ _ _ _ _

SPLaT sudoku

Find the missing stickers to finish the grid. There can only be one of each splat in every row and column.

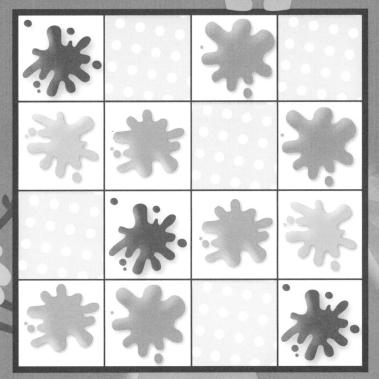

Use colour to finish the patterns.

ROTTEN rathers

WOULD YOU RATHER...

Pour a bucket of slugs over your head ☐
or
eat a snail sandwich? ☐

Drink a pint of bathwater ☐
or
drink a pint of pond water? ☐

Lie on a bed of nails ☐
or
lie on a bed of worms? ☐

Run around school in your underwear ☐
or
have six school detentions? ☐

Sit in a bath of snakes ☐
or
give a tarantula a bath? ☐

Fill your pockets with cockroaches ☐
or
fill your shoes with maggots? ☐

24

SNaiL trail

Find your way through the trail. Collect all the snails along the way and avoid the slime puddles!

Start

Finish

How many snails did you collect? Write the answer. ....

SPLAT box

Keep your splat safe
in a stinky haven.

1 Press out the splat box shape
and open the slots either side
of the ankle and toes.

slot

2 Fold along the creases.

3 Slot one toe on top of
the other. Then, do the
same at the ankle end.

4 You should now have
a box shape!

5 Finish the box with stickers.

LaVa Land

This is a game for two players.

Instructions:

1. Press out the mouthpiece and three target volcanoes from the card pages.

2. Curl each volcano into a cone shape and glue the sides together, as shown.

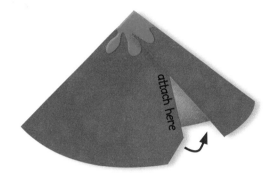

attach here

3. Cut out this page. Turn it over to see the Lava Land board and lay it flat on a table.

4. Tape the volcanoes into place on the board. You now have three volcano islands.

How to play:

• Players take turns dropping the splat through the mouth piece onto one of the volcano targets. Each target has a set number of points (10, 20 or 30). Keep score on a separate piece of paper.

• If the splat lands in the lava, the player gets 0 points.

• The player with the highest score after five turns, wins!

VOLCANO
10 POINTS

VOLCANO
20 POINTS

VOLCANO
30 POINTS